# Small Group Leader's Guide

SHANNYN CALDWELL

Copyright © 2015 Heavens to Betsy Press

All rights reserved.

ISBN: 0692426337
ISBN-13: 978-0692426333

# ACKNOWLEDGMENTS

I'm sure you've heard the African proverb "It takes a village to raise a child." Well, I think we can all agree that is the plain truth.

*The Healing Season* has been nurtured and loved, and in large ways, birthed by a truly amazing village of believers. You should also know that everyone who has had a hand in the creation of this series is a sold out follower of Jesus. We are pretty much on fire, and that's why we are doing this! We hope it's catchy and that you find what we have found and continue to find…a season of healing. We've been praying hard for you. Pastor Jim Pool (who really came up with the idea of *The Healing Season*) has been praying for you.

Mary Grace Donahue, who led the first *40-Day Healing Season* small group at the Renaissance Vineyard Church in Ferndale Michigan, has been praying for you, too. My husband, Joseph and I…we pray for you who the Lord would connect with this tool, that you would have a deep encounter with the living God. That He would move in a profound way and that revival would just break right OUT!

Yep. We are praying for revival. And speaking of my husband, Joseph, I would like to thank Joseph David Caldwell for giving me all the freedom, help and support I needed to pursue what God is doing in the *Healing Season*, from its start until today and beyond.

In fact a lot of hands and hearts went into the creation of this series. Here is the outrageous collection of talented people I'm humbled to say joined us in that vision and worked on the *40-Day Healing Season Small Group Series*.

Derek Carlson of DJames Videography for directing, editing and creating an overall vision for this radio girl who doesn't dream in pictures. Thank you, DJ, for seeing and believing and working in this field. You…just…rock.

Jason Roche-Film University Detroit Mercy shot most of the video and stayed up loading files until like 3 am. He paid for more space on his personal Dropbox to get the files to DJ. Jason's directed an award-winning film about Tiger Stadium. It's called *Stealing Home*. The website is www.stealinghomedetroit.com. Check it out!

ReShawn Wilder shot the video of Tom and Mary and prayed up a mighty prophetic storm. I'm so thankful for this man of God (he's young and super cute, by the way).

Britney Smith (who is also super cute and young) dropped everything after church on Sunday to come hold an umbrella in the air so that snow didn't hurt Jason's camera.

Patricia Sabino Krupuske did my makeup in video you don't get to see, but I looked fabulous!

Joy McMillan of Simply Bloom does my graphics. Aren't they GORGE?

KC Griffith helps me with social media...and plays hockey like a boss. But not just that, she's been praying for this project for years now. Thanks, girl.

You, too Megan Pool! Megan gave me my first Bible and has been the most steadfast of friends.

Plus...these BROWNIES?

Are you KIDDING me, right now?

Susan and Tricia and Bonnie and Kelly. Prayer warriors!

My mentor, Nancy Rue is the reason this thing stays on the rails! Thank you, Jesus, for my mentor NANCY RUE! (you guys, she mentors writers and believe me...it really helps! Nancyrue.com)

To my friend and teacher, Courtney Chalfant of Yahweh Yoga, thank you. For more on Christian yoga and meditation, www.yahwehyoga.com.

My editor on this leg of the *Healing Season* project is Kelly Hawkins. What a pro. What a gift. How wonderful it is to hand over something you love so dearly with the words, "I trust you." Thank you, Kelly!

Yvette Turmaine and Steve Cook, thank you for letting us shoot at the glorious and heavenly Tantra Aveda Spa in Ferndale.

Tom and Mary Quinlan are in this video, too.

That is a true honor.

If ever I've seen Jesus in someone, it's surely in them.

And when I saw Him, I was healed.

So, here we are,

excited and expectant

to see the hand of the Almighty reach down

and reach out, through the hands of the body of Christ

as we carry on the tradition of the fathers and mothers of our faith

and ask the Lord for His kingdom

now and here

and with us.

# A Note from Shannyn

Congrats on your bravery and following through on God's calling to lead your small group through this bold and searching 40-Day journey! Over the course of the next 6 weeks, you will be seeing the Holy Spirit move in power. You will see your skills of discernment sharpened. You will see bonds built that will have the potential to last a lifetime, because you and your group are about to go deep.

Going deep can be a scary thing, but I'm convinced, after talking now with more than a hundred others who have so far completed the 40-Day adventure that you and your group are embarking on, that living broken and surrendered to brokenness is also a scary proposition, indeed. What's more, God tells us in His Word that He has no intention of leaving us broken or orphaned. A truth which He has proven to me repeatedly and which I have chronicled for you in my book *The Healing Season: How a Deadly Tornado Wrecked and Reshaped My Faith*. If I could create for you a "package" for your small group study and your personal preparation, it would surely include a copy of that memoir, just for you, the leader, to read. If you can take the time to pick up the book (it's on Amazon and ShannynCaldwell.com plus select retail outlets), do so.

Read it. I'll make an audio version as soon as I can. Promise. Mostly, I ask that you are familiar with *The Healing Season* because the fight for my healing and reconciliation was just that. It was a fight, and a hard one. It involved a LOT of hard work and a lot of other people who prayed and fasted with me and my family and who were willing to go to extremes to press the kingdom of heaven into my bleak estate. I feel like it would be of real benefit for you, as the leader, to see exactly what was involved in *The Healing Season*, so that perhaps you can go in with some of the blinders off and the "warning label" read completely.

There will likely be spiritual attack on you and on the people in your group who are doing the work these 40-Days. Don't be surprised if problems begin to drop out of thin air. In fact, be encouraged. God wants us healed. The enemy wants us stuck, trapped, broken and shameful. For you fix your eyes on Jesus, the author and finisher of our faith.
He is with you.
He is for you and He is unstoppable.

But as much as I wish it were not so, the enemy is real and still fighting, and he has a history of kicking up a lot of dust as people walk through *The 40-Day Healing Season*. If it wasn't actually bringing Jesus's hope and healing, Satan wouldn't bother. I just don't want you to be surprised.

If you should find yourself thinking you could use some spiritual back up, please don't hesitate. Connect with your pastor or (if you are the pastor) connect with church leadership whom you seek for Godly and wise prayer and counsel. Remember…we are the body of Christ, and these next few weeks will show you how much our connection to one another is key to our connection to Jesus and to seeing His kingdom draw near.

Your group serves several purposes. It helps its members stay on track through their 40-Day Healing Season, it connects the members with their prayer partners and it builds community. Speaking of

# THE HEALING SEASON

## SMALL GROUP LEADER'S GUIDE

community, please consider inviting friends from outside your church who may benefit from this. If the people from the Vineyard would not have invited me to their small group, well, none of this would have happened. At least not the way it did.

After your group's time of fellowship (hanging out and eating together) and worship (singing songs of praise to God either with a live musician or live recorded music), next you'll play the video. They are all roughly 30 minutes in length.

The first half is a teaching. I'll share with you some tools and help you practice with them. You'll meet many of the people who were instrumental in the creation of *The Healing Season* and they will share their expertise and insight on the weekly focus.

The second half of the video is a prayer timing clock which will allow your group to break into pairs and pray for one another about their tornados. The clock back-times 15 minutes. A subtle bell with ring at 7 minutes 30 seconds into prayer time, but you will be responsible for asking your group to switch rolls at the half way point. That's when you will ask the person who is praying to wrap up and switch to the person being prayed for.

Note: Your group will likely want to chat and catch up instead of cutting right to praying about their tornado. Please, do them and yourself a favor and keep them on track. Remind them that they will have time to catch up soon, but now it's prayer time, and make sure they are only praying about the tornado that was chosen for these 40 days.

If you and your group want to have a more open prayer time when you close, you are obviously free to do so, but for the purpose of *this* prayer time…pray about the tornados. You are going to go after that same tornado again and again until all the debris is cleared!

I've added a couple of "bonus prizes" for you and your group as well. At the beginning of each week, you'll find "Seasoning with Mary Grace". Mary Grace Donahue is the first person in the world to lead a *Healing Season* small group, which she bravely led for Lent (2015) at the Renaissance Vineyard Church in Ferndale, Michigan, and she's kindly added her reflections to help you along your journey. Throughout these 40 days, you will (if your group is really honest and real) surely see God move. Perhaps He will move in ways that you've never seen or never expected. So, in the same way the airline pilot calls to the plane behind him to tell of the conditions, Mary Grace will tell you "about the weather" she experienced as they flew among tornados.

One thing that struck me as someone outside the church looking in, was the way this group "bore one another's burdens." They shared everything and it made their lives light and easy.

One way that was clearly taught to me was in the way that they did small group.
Acts 2:45-47 says, *They broke bread in their homes and ate together with glad and sincere hearts, praising God and enjoying the favor of all people. And the Lord added to their number daily those who were being saved.*

The other bonus prize I have for you is *recipes!* Well, menu's mostly. But recipes, too, from the amazing women you meet in *The Healing Season!*

The small groups I attended in *The Healing Season* broke bread together every week. But the burden was light because they did it in a simple way. They shared the burden. For example, Taco Night. Your group will have a host—the person at whose house you meet. In *The Healing Season*, that was Rebecca. The host may provide the browned taco meat or tempeh…a protein. Then another person brings the taco shells. Another, salsa. One cheese. So that when you put it all together, you have a full on feast, but no one spent more than $5 for their whole family. It's a total win, in my book. It made it really easy for me to say "Yes. I'll come with my son." I didn't have to think about cooking for one night. I just had to grab some salsa and come. And I know that I would be prayed for. And at the end of the day, don't we all desperately need to be prayed for?
And if a taco is going to get us to our knees…run to the border!

THE HEALING SEASON

SMALL GROUP LEADER'S GUIDE

I suggest you have coffee!
So, I thought I'd share it with *you!*

Don't feel as though you must employ the meal menus, but they are tried and true and there for you if you need them.
I've been intentional in selecting and creating healing choices for your group.
They are not all vegetarian or vegan, but I include that option.
Let's be honest, Christians are known on the street as poor tippers and bad eaters, and we need to be changing that because it makes us look like hypocrites and thereby discredits the King of Kings.
We can do better.

That said, Megan Pool's brownies are off the chain and absolutely HAD to be included in this book. Do yourself a giant favor **and make them for your first meeting**. I bring them up in the DVD and wouldn't it be too much fun to be eating them when the subject of the brownies comes up?
I know.
Mind.
Blown.

SHANNYN CALDWELL

# Megan's Mud Brownies

Megan credits this recipe to her friend Brooks Herning

### Ingredients
1 cup butter
½ cup cocoa
2 cups sugar
4 eggs
1 tsp vanilla
Pinch of salt
1 ½ cups flour
1 bag mini-marshmallows

### Frosting
1 pound box of confectioner's sugar
½ cup milk
1/3 cup cocoa
½ cup butter, softened

### Directions
Preheat the oven to 350°
Melt the butter, sugar and cocoa together on stovetop and then turn off the heat.
Add the eggs, vanilla, salt and stir well.
Add the flour and pour into the greased 9 x 13 pan.
Bake for 25-35 minutes.

### For the frosting
Cream together all four frosting ingredients.
Sprinkle the bag of marshmallows on top of the hot cake.
Spread the frosting over the marshmallows and stir the mixture slightly together.
Let sit for 20 minutes before serving.
Note: This is not a healthy recipe.

# Shannyn's Dark Chocolate Black Bean Brownies

**Yield:** 10-12 servings

## Ingredients

1  15.5 oz. can black beans, thoroughly rinsed and drained
½ tsp baking powder
½ cup + 1 Tbsp sugar or Xylitol
¼ cup dark cocoa powder
3 eggs
3 Tbsp olive oil
1 tsp vanilla
1 tsp instant coffee granules or 1 shot of espresso
¼ cup walnuts, chopped, optional
1/3 cup dark chocolate chips, more if you like

## Directions

Preheat oven to 350°. Grease the bottom of an 8 x 8 pan.
Place all the ingredients except chocolate chips and walnuts in a food processor or blender and pulse thoroughly until smooth and well combined.
Pour batter in the baking dish. Top with nuts and chocolate chips.
Bake for 30-35 minutes or until the top is dry and edges begin to pull away from the baking dish.
Cool completely before cutting.

Note: This is a relatively healthy and super delish gluten free choice to serve.

# CONTENTS

A Note from Shannyn   v

Week One—Your Story Matters   15

Week Two—Praying with a Friend   23

Week Three—Meditate on Meditation   31

Week Four—Learning to Hear the Still Small Voice   39

Week Five—Walking by Faith   47

Week Six—Finishing Strong   55

House Group Meal Ideas   61

SHANNYN CALDWELL

# WEEK ONE
## *Your Story Matters*

They triumphed by the blood of the Lamb and by the word of their testimony...

Revelation 12:11

# Seasoning with Mary Grace

*Your Story Matters!*

*"As a leader you are given the opportunity to share your story! You are fully capable of leading this small group. As you continue to put your trust in Jesus and allow him to work in your life, that is all that you need to both share and encourage others along the way."*

THE HEALING SEASON
SMALL GROUP LEADER'S GUIDE

## DAILY SUGGESTED FLOW:

This is an outline for an evening group, but you can adapt it to a morning or midday group.

6:00 p.m. Group Starts.

Have a time for hanging out, eating, drinking and catching up hereafter referred to as "fellowship."

6:30-6:45 Tidy up and transition to singing a couple of worship songs either with a friend who plays the guitar and sings lead or with some songs on CD.
That may feel a little strange at first, but believe me…it is powerful, powerful stuff that worship. It changes your heart and that is, after all, what we are here to do these 40-Days. So, worship! You don't have to raise your hands. You don't have to stand or dance. You only have to let the music soak you and let your heart turn, like a sunflower, toward the Son. Even if you just sing a few you all know. I mean, everyone knows *Amazing Grace*, right?
Right.
So…3-4 songs, just to get your hearts centered on Christ.
Hereafter referred to as "worship."

7:00 p.m. Start DVD teaching of the week.
The DVD segment includes a **15 minute prayer**

**timer.** This will allow your group to stay focused while praying together. You will, as the leader, want to tell them when they've reached the half way point (7 minutes 30 seconds into the prayer time) and ask them to switch rolls. The "prayer" becomes the "prayee" and vice versa.

7:30 Wrap up the time with prayer partners and gather back together to discuss the **closing questions** and pick next week's **menu assignments.**

8:00 p.m. Closing Prayer.
If there are any "loose ends" which need to be prayed for as a group, this is the time. Either that, or just a quick "Thanks, God. We love you!" words!

Goodnight and God bless!

THE HEALING SEASON

SMALL GROUP LEADER'S GUIDE

# Week One: *Your Story Matters* Conversation Starters:

\*Has everyone selected their tornados?

\*Let's talk about the "empty broken spot." Is this language making sense to you? How about those three deep breaths you take while inviting God into the emptiness? Does that make sense?

\*Ask them to share their tornados if they are willing.

\*How long have you been living with the wreckage of your tornado?

\*What are some ways it's affected your life? Your health? Your relationships?

\*Ask your group if anyone would like to share their picture of what their life would be like when they clear the debris and heal?

\*Is there anyone (including yourself) that it would be beneficial to forgive or to whom you may want to ask forgiveness before moving on?

*Discuss: If there are no *"miracles* too big or small for God," are there tornado's that are too big or small?

Teachers note:
If anyone says they don't have that empty broken spot…they should consider themselves blessed. Not everyone has it, but in the last year of teaching *Healing Season* workshops to hundreds of people, I've only met two people who authentically had no discernable brokenness. Yet, each of them had tornados. If your group member does not have an "empty broken" spot, PRAISE GOD!
Just get to the tornado and start clearing its debris.
You may also encounter someone who has "a lot" of tornados. Encourage them to choose ONE to work on for these 40 days.
They can always do another *Healing Season*.
But give each wound its chance to heal.
Clean it out.

# Extending the Table
*Recipes for Community Living*

Serve: Megan's Mud Brownies and sign up for:

## Giant Salad Bar

Host provides big bowl of shredded lettuces and spinach and dressing.

### Others sign up to bring:
Cubed green or red pepper
Cubed tomato and cucumber
Cheese, shredded
Garbanzo beans
Chopped hard boiled eggs
Olives, broccoli, onions or croutons
Rolls (consider something sprouted or gluten free) and butter or oil

# WEEK TWO
## *Praying with a Friend*

*Is anyone among you in trouble? Let them pray. Is anyone happy? Let them sing songs of praise. Is anyone among you sick? Let them call the elders of the church to pray over them and anoint them with oil in the name of the Lord. And the prayer offered in faith will make the sick person well; the Lord will raise them up. If they have sinned, they will be forgiven. Therefore confess your sins to each other and pray for each other so that you may be healed. The prayer of a righteous person is powerful and effective.*

James 5:13-16

# Seasoning with Mary Grace

*Praying with a Friend*

*"Do the Healing Season yourself. This will give **you** personal experiences to share with your group as they begin this journey. In my opinion, this is the single best aspect of the Healing Season. Having a Pastor or a Mentor in your life—someone you can trust, that you are able to share and be vulnerable with—takes tremendous courage. Have someone that can provide you with both support and challenge, someone who will see you through this journey!"*

## DAILY SUGGESTED FLOW:

This is an outline for an evening group, but you can adapt it to a morning or midday group.

6:00 p.m. Food and Fellowship (host puts on water for tea or coffee to drink during DVD)

6:30-6:45 Worship

All help tidy up

7:00 p.m. Start DVD teaching of the week and transition to partner prayer

7:30 Closer conversation starters and pick next week's **menu assignments**

8:00 p.m. Closing Prayer

Goodnight and God bless!

THE HEALING SEASON

SMALL GROUP LEADER'S GUIDE

# Week Two: *Praying with a Friend* Conversation Starters:

\*Ask about the prayer time. Is there anything they would like to share?

\*Tom and Mary Quinlan suggest that before you should touch or "lay hands" on someone you are praying for, you should always what? (answer: ask permission)

\*What is a "word of knowledge"? How do you know that it is from the Lord?

\*The Bible says, "the prayer of a righteous person is powerful and avails much." (James 5:16) What have *you* seen God do in answer to prayer?

\*Tom Quinlan shares a story about a rabbit that was hit by a car. Tom says he prayed for the rabbit to be healed. The rabbit died. Why do you think that happened as Tom is a righteous man who believed healing was possible?

Teacher's note:
As much as it is possible, try to keep your group from always choosing the same prayer partner each week. If they must (for trust reasons) pray with only one specific person at your small group, try to direct them to have another prayer partner on the weekend. If their church has a prayer ministry, any member of that team is perfect.

The only thing that should always be consistent, is that ALL the prayer partners should be followers of Jesus. If you have someone in your group who is not a Christian, then I would suggest creating a group of three…YOU being the third, to stand in the gap and intercede on their behalf. Just explain that you don't have to be a Christian to do the *Healing Season*, but that your prayers need to be exclusively and specifically to Jesus, as He is the healer.
This should not be offensive. If it is, just pray.
God is surely at work.
Ask Him for direction.
But, making a point of switching prayer partners should keep people from thinking that God hears one person more than another and from attributing their healing to the partner and not the Lord. It will also keep a prayer partner from burning out.

# Extending the Table
*Recipe for Community Living*

Serve: Giant Salad Bar and sign up for:

## Chicken (or Tofu) Curry

Main person brings diced chicken breasts or pressed tofu sautéed in onions, oil and curry spice mix of your choice.

### Others sign up to bring:

Rice (brown basmati or jasmine if you have it)
Julienned cucumber strips
Julienned carrot sticks
Chutney
Chopped green onions
Pineapple chunks
Chopped peanuts

*Put some protein on a bed of rice and top with any or all of the above.*

# WEEK THREE

*Meditate on Meditation*

*You will keep in perfect peace those whose minds are steadfast, because they trust in you.*

Isaiah 26:3

# Seasoning with Mary Grace

*Meditate on Meditation*

*"Pray. I'm very serious. Pray for people to sign up. Pray about the things you will share. Pray for each member of your group every day, and take the time to listen. For Week Three - Meditate on Meditation, each day there is a verse to meditate on. If in praying we ask, in meditation we receive."*

## DAILY SUGGESTED FLOW:

Note: This week you'll want to pop to the grocery store and pick up a bag of raw almonds. You'll be using them with the video! In the video, I do not say "take out your almond," etc. in case you didn't have time to run to the store, but when I bring up the almonds, just follow along.

6:00 p.m. Food and Fellowship
All help tidy up…host makes coffee or tea following meal

6:30-6:45 Worship

7:00 p.m. Start DVD teaching of the week and transition to partner prayer

7:30 Closer conversation starters and pick next week's **menu assignments**

8:00 p.m. Closing Prayer

Goodnight and God bless!

THE HEALING SEASON

SMALL GROUP LEADER'S GUIDE

# Week Three:
## *Meditate on Meditation*
# Conversation Starters:

\*Ask if there is anyone who thinks Meditation should not be practiced by Christians and have that conversation if you need to.

Here are some scriptures which support the idea of Christian Meditation
Psalms 19:14, 1:2, 48:9, 77:12, 119:15, 119:27, 119:48
There are many, many more.

\*What are simple things you do that could become meditations?
(walking, cleaning, reading the Bible)

\*Now, practice Lectio Divina with Psalm 119. You will need about 15-20 minutes to give the group a chance to really chew on and process this Psalm and this technique.
It's ideal to print out a copy for the group, in case they don't bring their Bibles.

## **The steps of Lectio Divina:**
Learn more in *Christian Yoga: Restoration for Body and Soul - An illustrated Guide to Self-Care* by Courtney Chalfant of *Yahweh Yoga*

### 1-Lectio
Read the scripture aloud, slowly, carefully and

several times. Consider words and phrases that catch your attention.

## 2-Meditatio

Spend some time reflecting on the passage. Ask questions, use your imagination. Meditation moves truth from the head to the heart. Allow your heart, attitudes, emotions to be subject to the probing of the Word, to be tested by the truth.

## 3-Oratio

After ingesting and internalizing the scripture, return it to the Lord in prayer. Personalize the scripture and bring it back to God in praise and petition. Praise Him for His work in you and ask Him for the grace for obedience.

## 4-Contemplatio

The final stage is resting and silence in the presence of God. This time of communion is the result of the first three stages and acknowledges that it is God at work in us, transforming our hearts and conforming us to His image.

# Extending the Table
*Recipe for Community Living*

Serve: Chicken (or Tofu) Curry and sign up for:

## Baked Potato Bar
Host provides baked potatoes

**Others sign up to bring:**
Shredded cheddar cheese
Sour cream or plain Greek yogurt
Butter and chopped chives
Steamed broccoli
Chili
Crumbled bacon, turkey bacon or smoked tempeh
etc.

*Top potatoes with some or all of the above.*

# WEEK FOUR

*Learning How to Hear the Still, Small Voice*

*Whether you turn to the right or to the left, your ears will hear a voice behind you, saying, "This is the way; walk in it."*

Isaiah 30:21

# Seasoning with Mary Grace

*Learning How to Hear the Still, Small Voice*

*"Create a comfortable environment to host your small group. This will help everyone as they are learning in Week Four – Learning How to Hear the Still, Small Voice. (We held our small group in my office with a renovation in progress, maybe not the most comfortable space.) Any space will do; when I say create the space, always arrive early to welcome your friends and have enough chairs available for everyone to sit down, and offer something to drink or eat. Many people will take initiative to help create this environment, and others will catch on. Encourage others to help create this kind of culture."*

## DAILY SUGGESTED FLOW:

6:00 p.m. Food and Fellowship
All help tidy up…host makes coffee or tea following meal

6:30-6:45 Worship

7:00 p.m. Start DVD teaching of the week and transition to partner prayer

7:30 Closer conversation starters and meditation
Pick next week's **menu assignments**

8:00 p.m. Closing Prayer

Goodnight and God bless!

# Week Four: *Learning How to Hear the Still, Small Voice* Conversation Starters:

*Ask the group to name some of the ways that we hear from God
*(His Word, other believers, dreams, words of knowledge, images, "God winks", a song on the radio at the right time, etc.)*

*Talk about "the heart shaped rock" we share about. How did Pastor Jim say that we knew it was more than a rock, but instead it was the Lord? (It came with a word or an "otherly" understanding.)

*How would you know it's NOT the voice of God you are hearing?
*(It will conflict with scripture. God will never go against His Word.)*

*Ask the group if anyone would like to share a time they know that they heard from God.

Teacher's Note: As you have your closing prayer time today, specifically pray that you will hear from the Lord. That He will "turn your antennas" to hear Him more clearly and more regularly and that you will have the strength to be open and obedient to what He speaks to your hearts.

THE HEALING SEASON

SMALL GROUP LEADER'S GUIDE

# Extending the Table
*Recipe for Community Living*
Serve: Baked Potato Bar and sign up for:

## Breakfast for Dinner
Host provides scrambled eggs

### Others sign up for:
Greek yogurt and honey
Oatmeal and brown sugar
Fresh fruit (diced)
Toast (consider wheat free, sprouted)
Juices

SHANNYN CALDWELL

# WEEK FIVE

*Walking by Faith*

For we live by faith, not by sight.

2 Corinthians 5:7

# Seasoning with Mary Grace

*Walking by Faith*

*"Take the time to watch the Healing Season small group videos. These were tremendously helpful as a way to start group. The videos will answer many questions about the weekly topic. We have the tools available, use them! We always watched the video and that filled us with great hope!"*

## DAILY SUGGESTED FLOW:

6:00 p.m. Food and Fellowship
All help tidy up…host makes coffee or tea following meal

6:30-6:45 Worship

7:00 p.m. Start DVD teaching of the week and transition to partner prayer

7:30 Closer conversation starters and pick next week's **menu assignments**

8:00 p.m. Closing Prayer

Goodnight and God bless!

THE HEALING SEASON

SMALL GROUP LEADER'S GUIDE

# Week Five: *Walking by Faith* Conversation Starters:

\*Aside from Jesus, what are some other places people put their faith?
*(job, stock market, fitness, their own strength, etc.)*

\*Why did Joseph say that he wanted to give his life to Jesus?

\*What could have happened to Joseph and Shannyn if Joe continued to keep his heart hard toward Jesus?

\*Whose marriage can this group, as a community, bless and support?

\*How were other people affected by Joseph's profession of faith?

\*What outward step did Joseph make?

\*Why would someone choose to get baptized or to make a public commitment to Christ?
(Follow up by asking if there is anyone who would like to get baptized at your Week 6 Party. If so, set up a preparatory meeting with your Pastor if need be and schedule a place to do the baptism(s).

Teachers Note: You can find the link to the video of Joseph's baptism at shannyncaldwell.com on the Healing Season tab. Feel free to share the video at some point either during your meeting tonight or even in an online page you or your group has to keep in touch.

Remember…Joseph was baptized in a baby pool on Main Street, so don't go crazy trying to find a proper place.)

# Extending the Table
*Recipe for Community Living*
Serve: Breakfast for dinner and sign up for:

# Thanksgiving Dinner

This will be your last week meeting for your *Healing Season* small group.

This last meeting should be a party and celebration (and maybe baptism). For next week, the host provides drinks and either a turkey breast or turkey. (Vegetarians can serve another delicious protein choice.)

**Others sign up to bring:**
Mashed Potatoes and/or Sweet Potatoes (consider creating a healthy version of these with coconut oil instead of butter)
Green beans or green bean casserole
Can of cranberries or fresh cranberry sauce
Rolls and butter
Tossed green salad
Corn
Stuffing
Pumpkin pie

## *My Mother's recipe for*
# Fresh Cranberry Orange Relish
### (by Shannyn Caldwell)

*note: Mom was diabetic. This is a low sugar recipe and it makes it to my Thanksgiving table every year per my children's request.*

## Ingredients:
1 bag of fresh cranberries
1 orange (quartered and seeds removed)
¼ cup of raw honey
¼ cup unsweetened applesauce

Place the cranberries and orange in the food processor and pulse until the desired consistency is reached. Some prefer a more coarse chop, while others choose a near puree. It's your choice.
*(Mom's was finely chopped.)*
When finished processing, transfer the mixture to a glass or plastic bowl. Mix in the honey and applesauce until they are well combined. Best if refrigerated overnight.

*Note: When this is almost gone, it's great mixed with mayo as a sandwich spread.*

# WEEK SIX
*Finishing Strong*

…my only aim is to finish the race and complete the task the Lord Jesus has given me—the task of testifying to the good news of God's grace.

Acts 20:24

# Seasoning with Mary Grace

*Finishing Strong*

*"What is God telling you? Did you skip a day? When you were journaling did God reveal something else? Take time to reflect on your work. This is your Healing Season."*

# DAILY SUGGESTED FLOW:

6:00 p.m. Food and Fellowship
All help tidy up...host makes coffee or tea following meal

6:30-6:45 Worship

7:00 p.m. Start DVD teaching of the week and transition to partner prayer

7:30 Closer conversation starters

8:00 p.m. Closing Prayer

Goodnight and God bless!

*Note: If you do choose to have baptisms of another outward profession of faith, do so before the food and fellowship! This is a celebration of Thanksgiving!*

# Week Six: *Finishing Strong* Conversation Starters:

*Looking back on these 40-Days, what have you seen God do?

*What was the hardest part of *The Healing Season* for you?

*Was there a time you were inclined to quit *The Healing Season*? If so, what propelled you onward?

*Is there any other tornado in your life that could use a healing season?

*What practices from these 40-Days would you like to carry into the future?

*Why do you think God chooses to seek us out in our brokenness? Why do you think He heals us?

*If you could go back to Day 1 and give yourself some advice or encouragement about the journey you were embarking on, what would it be?

Teacher's Note: I understand that you may love using the Extending the Table format but not really WANT "Curry Night," so here are a few more choices to fill your tummies while Jesus works on filling your other empty spots.

# Extending the Table
*Even MORE recipes for community living*

**Soup Bar Night:** Everyone brings their favorite soup.

**Pasta Bar Night:** Everyone brings a pot of their favorite pasta and/or sauce. Remember: there are lots of pastas, including black bean, kelp noodle and zucchini not to mention wheat and gluten free choices, so pasta night can still be healthy!

**Smoothie Bowl Night:** Host provides Greek yogurt. Others bring fresh fruit, granola, chopped nuts, honey, mint leaves

**Sandwich Bar Night:** Host provides protein (meat, smoked tofu or tempeh, veggie burgers). Others bring bread, mustard and mayo, lettuce, tomatoes, pickles, onions, etc.
For a healthier option, think about making lettuce wraps instead of using bread.

**TV Dinner Night:** Everyone brings their favorite TV dinner to enjoy.

**Hometown Food Night:** Everyone brings a dish that reminds them of home.

**Birthday Blessing Night:** If someone in the group is having a Birthday during *The Healing Season*, work together to make a special meal for that person.

**Healing Foods Night:** Everyone brings a dish that makes them feel healthier when eating.

**Appetizer Night:** Everyone brings their favorite appetizer. Examples: Hummus and pita chips, Veggie Tray, Bruschetta, Cheese and crackers, Bite-sized quiches, Mini egg rolls, Pretzels and assorted mustards.

The possibilities are endless.

Have FUN!

Be Well.

Be His.

Be Healed.

# Ordering Information

*The Healing Season: How a Deadly Tornado Wrecked and Reshaped My Faith, The 40-Day Healing Season, The Healing Season Small Group DVDs* and *Leader's Guide* by Shannyn Caldwell are available on Amazon and Kindle, **ShannynCaldwell.com** and retail outlets nationwide.

For Information on Healing Season Workshops, DVD series', resources and printables or to invite Shannyn to speak at your event, email
Shannyn@shannyncaldwell.com

Stay connected to the Healing Season community online:
www.facebook.com/healingseason (book series page)
www.facebook.com/40DayHealingSeason (closed supportive group for people doing the 40-Day Healing Season)
Instagram, Twitter, and Periscope
@shannyncaldwell
#healingseason

Made in the USA
Middletown, DE
31 October 2015